Built for Cold
Arctic Animals

Sled Dog

Powerful Miracle

by Stephen Person

Consultant: Diane Johnson, Director
Iditarod Education Department

BEARPORT PUBLISHING

New York, New York

Credits

Cover and Title Page, © Robert McGouey/Alamy; TOC, © Cherevko/Shutterstock; 4, © The Canadian Press/ Jonathan Hayward; 5, © The Canadian Press/Jonathan Hayward; 6, © The Canadian Press/Jonathan Hayward; 7, © The Canadian Press/Jonathan Hayward; 8, © The Granger Collection, New York; 9L, © Julie Konop/ Exploratorium/www.exploratorium.edu; 9R, © M. Watson/Ardea; 10L, © Wolfgang Kaehler/Corbis; 10R, © Nathaniel Wilder/Reuters/Landov; 11, © Accent Alaska/Alamy; 12T, Courtesy of Alaska State Library/ William Norton Photograph Collection; 12B, © The Protected Art Archive/Alamy; 13, Courtesy of Alaska State Library/Sadlier-Olsen Family Photograph Collection; 14T, © Carrie McLain Museum/AlaskaStock; 14B, © Carrie McLain Museum/AlaskaStock; 15L, © Cal Vornberger/Alamy; 15R, © Terrence Spencer/Time Life Pictures/Getty Images; 16, © Bryan & Cherry Alexander/Arcticphoto; 17, © Nathaniel Wilder/Reuters/ Landov; 18, © Robert Maier/Animals Animals Enterprises; 19L, © Klein & Hubert/Bios/Photolibrary; 19C, © Lynn Stone/Animals Animals Enterprises; 19R, © Lynn Stone/Animals Animals Enterprises; 20T, Courtesy of Cascade Kennel; 20B, © Steven J. Kazlowski/Alamy; 21, © Loren Holmes/Accent Alaska; 22T, © William R. Sallaz/Sports Illustrated/Getty Images; 22B, © Jeff Schultz/Alaska Stock/Alamy; 23, © Jeff Schultz/Alaska Stock; 24, © AP Images/Ilnar Salakhiev; 25L, © Jeff Schultz/Alaska Stock; 25R, © Carl Auer/NewSport/ Corbis; 26, © Jeff Schultz/Alaska Stock/Alamy; 27, © AP Images/Bob Hallinen/Anchorage Daily News; 28, © Sirko Hartmann/Shutterstock; 29TL, © All Canada Photos/SuperStock; 29TR, © F1 ONLINE/SuperStock; 29B, © All Canada Photos/SuperStock; 31, © Ventura/Shutterstock; 32, © Marcel Jancovic/Shutterstock.

Publisher: Kenn Goin
Editorial Director: Adam Siegel
Creative Director: Spencer Brinker
Photo Researcher: Daniella Nilva

Library of Congress Cataloging-in-Publication Data

Person, Stephen.
  Sled dog : powerful miracle / by Stephen Person.
    p. cm. — (Built for cold: arctic animals)
  Includes bibliographical references and index.
  ISBN-13: 978-1-61772-134-2 (library binding)
  ISBN-10: 1-61772-134-4 (library binding)
  1. Sled dogs—Juvenile literature. I. Title.
  SF428.7.P47 2011
  636.73—dc22
                          2010041165

For more information, write to Bearport Publishing Company, Inc., 45 West 21st Street, Suite 3B, New York, New York 10010. Printed in the United States of America in North Mankato, Minnesota.

10 9 8 7 6 5 4 3

Contents

Isobel's Story

It was a sunny winter day in 2005 near the town of Churchill, Canada. A team of dogs was pulling a sled along a snowy trail. They were **training** for a race. Suddenly, a dog named Isobel began to **stagger**. Then she stopped and refused to start running again. Her owners, Gerald Azure and Jenafor Ollander, knew something was very wrong.

Isobel (on the right) was pulling a sled along a trail like this one when she came to a sudden stop.

They rushed Isobel to a **veterinarian**. The doctor discovered that Isobel had a disease that had caused her to go blind. Isobel's life as a sled dog was over, the doctor said. Gerald and Jenafor took Isobel home and kept her inside—but she did not like her new life. She seemed sad and even stopped eating and drinking. Her owners were afraid that unless they could figure out what was wrong, Isobel would soon die.

This photo shows Isobel after she went blind. She lost her sight when she was four years old.

Sled dog racing is a popular sport today. In short sprints, sled dogs like Isobel can reach speeds of about 28 miles per hour (45 kph).

Back on the Trail

Finally, Gerald and Jenafor realized that Isobel still wanted to run. They took her outside and **hitched** her up to the sled, along with her old team of racing dogs. Gerald climbed into the sled and shouted, "Let's go!" The dogs began to run. "The first couple of steps she stumbled a little bit," said Gerald. "After that it was straight on down the trail."

Isobel (on the left) helps lead her team of sled dogs. Isobel relies on the dog running beside her to help guide her in the right direction.

As soon as she began racing again, Isobel went back to being the high-energy, fun-loving dog she had been before. "She runs better now than she did with her eyesight," said Jenafor. Isobel's story is unusual, but she shares one important **trait** with sled dogs everywhere—a love of running.

Even after going blind, Isobel helped her team win several sled dog races. She retired from racing in January 2010, at the age of nine.

Isobel's story **inspired** many people. "She has touched the hearts of a lot of people," says Jenafor. "If a blind sled dog can run, just think of what the rest of the world can do!"

Dogs Move North

Sled dogs like Isobel have been helping people for thousands of years. Scientists believe that humans first **migrated** to the **Arctic region** with their dogs more than 25,000 years ago. With one of the coldest **climates** on Earth, the Arctic is not an easy place to live.

People in the Arctic began using dogs to pull sleds at least 3,000 years ago.

The Arctic region is the northernmost area on Earth.

ASIA
NORTH POLE
Arctic Ocean
EUROPE
Alaska
ARCTIC REGION
Pacific Ocean
NORTH AMERICA
Atlantic Ocean

Winter temperatures in the Arctic fall to −60°F (−51°C), and the land is covered with snow and ice for much of the year. **Native people** learned to use dogs to help them survive in the freezing landscape. The dogs pulled sleds over the snow, carrying people and supplies. They also warned people of nearby danger—like prowling polar bears.

Dogs helped people in the Arctic hunt. Using their strong sense of smell, dogs found breathing holes in the sea ice used by seals. Human hunters then waited by the holes. When seals came up to breathe, hunters caught the seals and brought the meat back to their families.

A seal coming up for air

Today, dogs are still used for hunting. They sniff out seals' breathing holes in the Arctic sea ice.

Two Coats for the Winter

Today's sled dog is a **descendant** of the earliest dogs that came to the Arctic. Over thousands of years, these dogs **adapted** to life in a very cold climate. For example, sled dogs have two coats of fur—an outer coat and an inner coat. The outer coat is long and shaggy, protecting dogs from the cold and wind. The inner coat is thick and **waterproof**. This keeps the dogs' skin dry, even when it's snowing.

Sled dogs have thick pads on the bottoms of their feet, which protect them from being damaged by ice or rocks.

In long races, sled dogs wear special booties to give their feet extra protection.

The dog's bushy tail also has an important job. When a dog curls up to sleep, it wraps its tail over its nose. As the dog breathes in, the furry tail warms the air. This keeps the dog's **lungs** from freezing while it sleeps.

Sled dogs sleep outside year-round, in all kinds of weather.

Sled dogs have large, flat feet. These help the dogs run on soft snow without sinking too much. Their toenails are strong and sharp—which is useful for traveling over ice without slipping.

Dogs of the Gold Rush

Native people of the Arctic were not the only ones to rely on sled dogs. In the late 1800s, miners found gold in Alaska and northern Canada. Thousands of people raced north with dreams of getting rich. In summer, they reached **remote** mining camps by riverboat. When the rivers froze in October, however, the only way to travel was by dog sled.

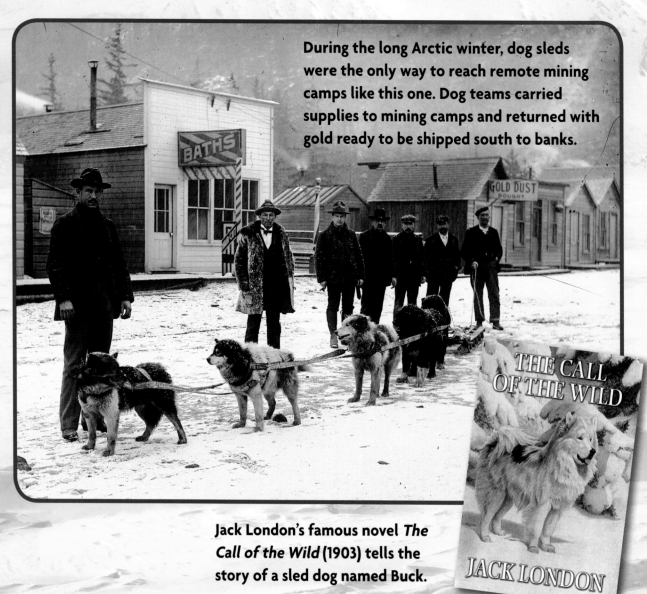

During the long Arctic winter, dog sleds were the only way to reach remote mining camps like this one. Dog teams carried supplies to mining camps and returned with gold ready to be shipped south to banks.

Jack London's famous novel *The Call of the Wild* (1903) tells the story of a sled dog named Buck.

Alaska's sled dog drivers soon established the Iditarod Trail, a 1,150-mile (1,851-km) trail winding from Seward to Nome. Teams of sled dogs carried mail and supplies to towns and mining camps along the trail. A 20-dog team could pull 1,000 pounds (454 kg) of people or **goods**.

These sled dogs helped deliver mail in Alaska.

The Iditarod

It took dog teams about three weeks to travel the Iditarod Trail from Seward to Nome. Historians believe that the name Iditarod comes from a Native American word meaning "distant place."

Sled Dogs to the Rescue

In January 1925, sled dogs carried more than mail and supplies. The deadly disease **diphtheria** was spreading among the children of Nome, Alaska. Without medicine, many would die—but the nearest medicine was in the town of Nenana, 674 miles (1,085 km) away. Planes could not fly safely in the freezing and snowy weather. Only sled dogs could reach the sick children in time.

Togo was one of the sled dogs that raced across Alaska. He was famous for his strength, courage, and ability to find the trail even in fierce snowstorms.

This team of sled dogs helped carry medicine to the sick children of Nome.

As temperatures fell to −40°F (−40°C), teams of dogs ran night and day toward Nome. Drivers and dog teams raced up to 50 miles (80 km) before handing the medicine to a fresh team. Less than six days after the first team left Nenana, a dog named Balto led a sled carrying the medicine into Nome. Balto and the other dogs had saved hundreds of lives.

This statue of Balto can be seen in New York City's Central Park.

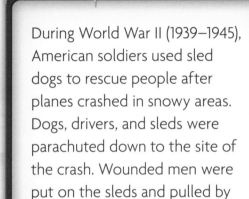

During World War II (1939–1945), American soldiers used sled dogs to rescue people after planes crashed in snowy areas. Dogs, drivers, and sleds were parachuted down to the site of the crash. Wounded men were put on the sleds and pulled by the dogs to the nearest town.

During World War II, special harnesses like this one were used to attach sled dogs to parachutes.

A New Race Begins

Balto and Togo helped make Alaska's sled dogs famous all over the world. New **technology**, however, soon started replacing these amazing animals. From the 1920s to the 1940s, airplanes and trucks began carrying mail and supplies across the Arctic. In the 1950s, people also started using snowmobiles in the Arctic. Like dogs, snowmobiles could travel over snowy, roadless areas—only snowmobiles were even faster. Was this the end of the sled dog?

Snowmobiles make it easy to travel quickly in the Arctic.

No, because the people of the Arctic loved sled dogs too much to let them disappear. People decided that if sled dogs were no longer needed for travel, they could be used for racing. This led to the rise of the popular sport of sled dog racing. The world's most famous sled dog race, the Iditarod, is held each March in Alaska.

Iditarod racers use teams of up to 16 dogs to pull their sleds. The best dog teams can average about 11 miles per hour (18 kph) over the entire race.

Founded in 1973, the Iditarod is a 1,049-mile (1,688-km) race from Anchorage to Nome. Much of the race follows the historic route of the Iditarod Trail.

Mutts Wanted

In races like the Iditarod, the driver is called a musher. Top mushers **breed** their own sled dogs. The three most popular sled dog breeds are the Siberian husky, the Alaskan malamute (MAL-uh-myoot), and the Samoyed (*sam*-uh-YEHD). The best sled dogs are often not **purebreds**, however. They are a mixture of breeds and are often simply called Alaskan huskies.

Alaskan huskies

When it comes to sled dogs, bigger does not mean better. The best racing dogs are about two feet (.6 m) high at the shoulder and weigh about 50 pounds (23 kg). Larger dogs can be stronger, but they are slower runners.

Sled dogs are bred to be fast and strong, with tough feet. They are very smart and work well as members of a team. Most important of all, the best dogs can't wait to get out on the snow and **compete**. "The dogs must have a love of running, and a never-say-die attitude," said champion musher Susan Butcher.

Sled Dog Breeds

BREED	Siberian husky	Alaskan malamute	Samoyed
HEIGHT AT SHOULDER	20–23.5 inches (51–60 cm)	23–25 inches (58–64 cm)	19–23.5 inches (48–60 cm)
WEIGHT	35–60 pounds (16–27 kg)	75–85 pounds (34–39 kg)	35–60 pounds (16–27 kg)
TRAITS	strong and fast, great **endurance**	very powerful, able to pull heavy sleds over long distances	tough feet, thick coat, works well in **extreme** cold

Trainers often mix these breeds, as well as others, to try to breed the best sled dogs.

Dogs and Mushers

When dogs are just a few months old, some mushers begin training them by having the dogs pull car tires around the yard. At six to eight months, a dog is ready to wear a **harness** and pull a sled on short runs. By about 18 months, a sled dog is ready to race.

This sled dog trains for racing by pulling a tire.

Sled dogs train all year, even when there's no snow on the ground. In summer, they stay strong by pulling carts instead of sleds.

The most important part of every sled team is the dog at the front of the team, known as the lead dog. A good lead dog can be either male or female, as long as he or she is fast and smart. Mushers don't use ropes to steer the sled—they just use their voices. As a result, lead dogs have to be able to understand and follow the musher's commands.

Here are some commands all lead dogs must learn:
"Let's go"—start running
"Gee"—turn right
"Haw"—turn left
"Easy"—slow down
"Whoa"—stop

Mushers form a close bond with their dogs when the animals are very young. Only dogs that love and trust their owners will make good racers.

Follow the Leader

Just how important is a great lead dog? Susan Butcher found out one winter day in 1977. While training with her team on a frozen river in Alaska, Susan yelled, "Haw!"—the command for "turn left." Susan's lead dog, Tekla, swerved sharply to the right. "She had never done anything wrong before," Susan said of Tekla. "I couldn't understand why she was disobeying me."

Susan Butcher and her dogs crossing a frozen lake

Susan Butcher with one of her sled dogs

Something told Susan to trust her lead dog. She let Tekla lead the team to the right. As the dogs and sled turned right, the ice to the left of them cracked and fell into the river. "Tekla had a **sixth sense** that saved our lives," Susan said.

Along the Iditarod course, mushers stop at 26 checkpoints so veterinarians, such as this one, can check each dog's health. If a dog is sick or injured, it must leave the race. Dogs that need quick medical attention are taken by plane to Anchorage.

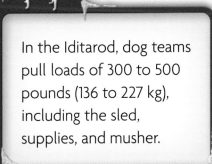

In the Iditarod, dog teams pull loads of 300 to 500 pounds (136 to 227 kg), including the sled, supplies, and musher.

Danger: Moose Crossing

No matter how well prepared a dog team is, there can be unexpected dangers on the trail. When the 1985 Iditarod began, Susan Butcher had the best team she'd ever put together. "No one was going to beat them or come close to beating them," Susan said.

Today sled dog races are held in many states besides Alaska and in several countries, including the United States, Norway, and Russia. This musher is racing his dogs near the Russian city of Novosibirsk.

On the second day of the race, Susan's dogs were in the lead. Then, as they sped around a curve in the trail, a giant moose jumped in front of the dogs. The moose charged at the dogs, kicking them with its powerful legs. Two of Susan's best dogs were killed, and many more were injured. She was forced to drop out of the race.

Libby Riddles won the 1985 Iditarod, becoming the first woman champion.

Susan Butcher returned in 1986 with her surviving dogs and a few new ones. She won the Iditarod that year—and again in 1987, 1988, and 1990.

Martin Buser (above) finished the 2002 Iditarod in record time—just 8 days, 22 hours, and 46 minutes.

The Dogs Come First

What's the secret to winning the Iditarod? It's simple, according to four-time champion Lance Mackey, who says, "I put my dogs first." In the 2010 Iditarod, crowds cheered wildly as Lance sped through the streets of Nome toward victory. Even then, Lance was thinking only of his dogs. "Nice, nice," he told them. "This is so cool. We're almost there, guys. You did such a good job!"

Lance crossing the finish line of the 2010 Iditarod

In 1978, Lance's father, Dick Mackey, won the closest Iditarod in history. Mackey's lead dog crossed the finish line just one second before the lead dog of second-place finisher Rick Swenson.

When he's not racing, Lance spends up to 19 hours a day training and caring for his dogs. Mushers get the fame and the prize money, but Lance knows that it's the dogs that win the race. After winning the 2010 Iditarod, Lance hugged each dog in his team, saying, "These are my heroes right here."

Lance with two of his dogs, Rev and Maple, that helped him win the 2010 Iditarod

Sled Dog Facts

Sled dogs have two layers of warm fur and a strong desire to run. This makes them perfectly adapted for pulling sleds across the Arctic snow. Here are some other facts about these smart and speedy animals.

Weight	The best racers are medium-size dogs—about 45 to 55 pounds (20 to 25 kg).
Height	19 to 25 inches (48 to 64 cm) from paw to shoulder
Food	Sled dogs burn huge amounts of energy on the trail. To keep running all day, they must eat a lot of food—about five times more than an average dog! Mushers feed their dogs a special mix of dog food, fresh meat, and vitamins.
Life Span	13 to 16 years
Habitat	Arctic region; today sled dogs are kept as pets in many parts of the world

More Arctic Animals

The Arctic region is one of the harshest **habitats** on Earth. Only animals that are adapted to extreme cold, such as sled dogs, can survive there. Here are two other Arctic survivors.

Snowshoe Hare

- The snowshoe hare's name comes from its wide, furry feet. These big feet help the hare travel over soft snow without sinking.
- During the summer, a snowshoe hare's fur is brown and gray. In the fall, the hare grows thick white fur that keeps it warm—and hidden from **predators**—during the snowy winter.

- Adult snowshoe hares usually weigh from 2.6 to 3.5 pounds (1.2 to 1.6 kg).
- Snowshoe hares can reach a speed of 27 miles per hour (43 kph). They can travel up to 10 feet (3 m) in a single jump.
- Snowshoe hares eat plants, berries, and tree bark.

Snowy Owl

- Snowy owls are about 20 inches (51 cm) tall, with a wingspan of almost 5 feet (1.5 m). They have an average weight of 4 to 5 pounds (1.8 to 2.3 kg).
- A thick layer of feathers covers the owl's entire body, including its legs and toes. The feathers keep the owl warm in temperatures as low as −58°F (−50°C).

- The owl's white feathers allow it to blend in with the snow. This helps the owl hunt without being seen by its **prey**.
- Snowy owls eat mouse-like animals called lemmings. They can also catch and kill hares, seabirds, and even foxes.

Glossary

adapted (uh-DAP-tid) changed over time to survive in an environment

Arctic region (ARK-tic REE-juhn) the northernmost area on Earth; it includes the Arctic Ocean, the North Pole, and northern parts of Europe, Asia, and North America, and is one of the coldest areas in the world

breed (BREED) to keep animals so that they can mate and produce young

climates (KLYE-mits) patterns of weather over a long period of time

compete (kuhm-PEET) to struggle against others to gain something

descendant (di-SEND-uhnt) a living thing that is related to other living things from the past

diphtheria (dif-THEER-ee-uh) a deadly disease that begins in the nose and throat; it is most dangerous to children under the age of 5 and adults over 60

endurance (en-DUR-uhnss) the ability or strength to continue despite bad conditions

extreme (ek-STREEM) very great or severe

goods (GUDZ) things that are sold

habitats (HAB-uh-*tats*) places in the wild where animals or plants normally live

harness (HAR-niss) a device attached to an animal that allows people to hold on to the animal

hitched (HICHT) fastened to something

inspired (in-SPIRED) was a good example and encouraged others to do something

lungs (LUHNGZ) parts of the body in a person's or an animal's chest that are used for breathing

migrated (MYE-*grayt*-id) moved from one place to another

native people (NAY-tiv PEE-puhl) people belonging to a particular place because of where they were born

predators (PRED-uh-turz) animals that hunt other animals for food

prey (PRAY) an animal that is hunted by another animal for food

purebreds (PYOOR-bredz) animals whose parents, grandparents, and other ancestors are all the same kind of animal

remote (ri-MOHT) far from any settled place; hard to reach

sixth sense (SIKSTH SENSS) the ability to sense something without using any of the five main senses of touch, taste, smell, sight, and hearing

stagger (STAG-ur) to stumble; to move on shaky legs

technology (tek-NOL-uh-jee) the use of science to do practical things

training (TRAYN-ing) practicing for a competition; learning new skills

trait (TRAYT) a quality or characteristic of a person or an animal

veterinarian (*vet*-ur-uh-NER-ee-uhn) a doctor who cares for animals

waterproof (WAH-tur-*proof*) something that does not allow water to pass through

Bibliography

Lance Mackey's Comeback Kennel, Inc.
(www.mackeyscomebackkennel.com/index.html)

The Official Site of the Iditarod
(www.iditarod.com/)

PBS/Nature ("Sled Dogs: An Alaskan Epic")
(www.pbs.org/wnet/nature/episodes/sled-dogs-an-alaskan-epic/
introduction/3146/)

Read More

Cary, Bob. *Born to Pull: The Glory of Sled Dogs*. Minneapolis, MN: University of Minnesota Press (2009).

Haskins, Lori. *Sled Dogs (Dog Heroes)*. New York: Bearport Publishing (2006).

Miller, Debbie S. *The Great Serum Race: Blazing the Iditarod Trail*. New York: Walker Publishing Company, Inc. (2002).

Whitelaw, Ian. *Snow Dogs! Racers of the North*. New York: Dorling Kindersley (2008).

Learn More Online

To learn more about sled dogs, visit
www.bearportpublishing.com/BuiltforCold

Index

About the Author

Stephen Person has written many children's books about history, science, and the environment. His childhood dog was half Siberian husky (and half poodle). He lives with his family in Saratoga Springs, New York.